The Dowry of Education

Previously published by Corrado Paina:

In Italian:
Di Corsa—Mapograph, 1996
Tempo Rubato—Atelier 14, 2003
Darsena Inquinata—Ulisse Editrice, 2004

In English:
Hoarse Legend—Mansfield Press, 2000

The Dowry of Education

Corrado Paina

Mansfield Press

Printed in Canada

Library and Archives Canada Cataloguing in Publication

Paina, Corrado, 1954 –
The dowry of education / Corrado Paina.

Poems.
ISBN 1-894469-20-8

I. Title.

PS8581.A4843D69 2004 C811'.6 C2004-905371-X

Design: Marijke Friesen
Cover Photo: Wonderfile

Acknowledgements

Descant: *Poemless Bus, Scent of Gods in Chinatown, Blue cake of dreams, Burning in my remaining years.*
Il ragazzo Innocuo (Milan): *My memories at four years old.*
LyricalMyrical: *Spies in Kensington, Tonight I am the State.*

The publication of *The Dowry of Education* has been generously supported by The Canada Council for the Arts and The Ontario Arts Council.

Mansfield Press Inc.
25 Mansfield Avenue, Toronto, Ontario, Canada M6J 2A9
Publisher: Denis De Klerck
www.mansfieldpress.net

Table of Contents

Preface

A few years ago while recovering from a long treatment, I discovered Nuevitas, an important little harbour in the economy of Cuba. Nuevitas was my *Macondo*, the place where I could have lived despite the malaise that I feel every time I am in Cuba. The island is beautiful, the nature is stunning, but the human beings are still suffering because of the endless debate between history and freedom. Is it better to be free or to be fed? This is an answer that only Cuban people can give and nobody else can pretend to give on their behalf.

My "mal de Cuba," ending *The Dowry of Education*, was conceived on Mansfield Avenue, in the basement of my little Canadian house, which is between a church and a schoolyard.

In the summer, when the swallows have left their embroidered nests under Portuguese and Italian roofs, the leaves of a few secular trees crown the park, hiding the view of a 1960's school, a barrack in concrete, with harlequinade walls recalling East Berlin architecture. There is a playground with a dry pool and a wooden bridge and swings with tires for the leisure of children.

It was there that I wrote this book, looking at the wall and at the computer screen, sometimes going to the park with my young daughter Andrea and my companion Deborah, to smoke a cigarette and relax after a shot of medication in my leg or arm. I had plenty of time to think and write about:

1. life threatening disease
2. Andrea growing purely and purely playing in the schoolyard
3. the dismantling of the playground by the workers of the city
4. drugs (so much has been meditated and written, but a humble fear was not enough to challenge my arrogance)
5. supreme faith and starvation

I lived in exile, isolated in particular from the nightlife of College Street, visited frequently by Italian and Canadian friends and by my beloved first publisher in Canada, who lived in a house in front of me, and who, in an excess of fancy, called his publishing house Mansfield Press.

I thank them and I hold them all responsible for this book.

The Conspiracy of Liquids and Cells

To Maria Francesca and Carlo

The conspiracy of liquids and cells

the cowl of the mist
hides the church
in a horrid placenta
bare ribs and a scoliotic roof
are exposed in mercenary impudence
the tumoral cyst of the bell tower rises fiercely

inside unto
the vaulted sternum
liquids cells
and experience flow unredeemed

words and teachings
all muted

the tabernacle pumps out solitude
it's a gelid pain

the moon hides her eyes
under the wing of the cloud

the sky is an archipelago of sailing lotus
of leaves blown over a sea of laudanum

the conspiracy keeps working restlessly
the liquids and the cells bury
intelligence and faith and hope
the mass will soon be over

Translation without dictionary

the night almost evaporated . . .
that neon foot soldier
denuding the pale cars
in front of the schoolyard

sounds of animals stirring
of adolescent rape
of alarm clocks

the awakening of the hobo
the drooling barking of the dog
the sacristan is still
under the somber vault
and he is thinking
then sighing

because of the repetitious torment
the dark dismembers itself

Poemless bus

there are buses without poems
perhaps because the passenger
is still dozing
there are buses without sounds
perhaps because there's too much thinking
not centric but
peripheral thought, that of
mad monads created
by the big bang of imploded mortgages
the black hole of a repetitive job
the marks of race
and so we all go
mute on a poemless, readerless, storytellerless bus
waiting for the stop where the adolescents
will bring their sparrow cries
of school homework and theoretical sex

Screening the flood

I am awake! I am listening!
my ear pressed at the wall of my skin
I know there are rivers
I can hear their foaming roar
the fragile rafts of life crashing
against debris of malignant fractions
and corpses floating
paying the price for their uprising

my ear can listen to the dark
my eyes can screen the greediness of
crowded pipelines or the abandoned carwash
in my intestine

pain is burning thorns in my
temples
racing on free highways

and fear
fear that everything will stop
and I will be the scab the lonely scab
in front of the large entrance to death

Toronto

I have been at times negligent
my eyes crawling with ingratitude
there were affairs with towns and remote cities
small squalid business

I go back sometimes to old love stories
just to hurt myself
I have been disloyal
lured into quick and forgettable infidelities
with bridges
rivers and churches

we lit a cigarette for each other
we had doorway sex
hiding from art and design
I thought they were looking for me

I invented forefathers and stepfathers
floating in a basket over the stream of
nostalgia

I am coming back to tell you
that my name is nobody
your only eye still raptured
and innocent

Scent of gods in Chinatown

flashes of dry monsters and shining devils
lit up by the cross-light
appear in the puddles spat
on the sidewalks
a dead crab lies on the road

that paragraph of flesh
of the careless pedestrian
is a loan of blood

I feel like a demigod
sent from the sky
to negotiate the prices

oh! Levantine market
I'm alive again
I'll be able to take away
sticky rice from the mother
of earth

even if I end like lost Diomedes
like a crab's corpse
for a moment
I smelled the scent of gods

Watermelon

Listen to the advice of the silent monolith. Inside there are sugary creatures. Screaming geysers of liquid glucose. Seed of blood sausages, viscera well laid out. You have killed its soul with a vulgar deed, cutting its extremities to violate its peace. You will be punished by a big wave that will swallow your screams. Listen when you knock on its walnut door to an apartment left by the tenants, and when lingering on the steps, imagine the children running. You will think you hear the happy shouts of games. This reconciled Red Sea is like a flag over a body. Inside the red planet there are hidden and loquacious springs where one can quench his thirst. Where one can bathe. Inside there is emptiness, like a box enveloped in precious tapestries, there is tepid light water, there's the sleep of the infant and the well's smell of its flower breath.

Losing my voice

my voice is not a voice
so feeble a voice
less than the whisper of the wind
lower than your cry
unborn blind spring
frozen in the throat of the mountain

my voice cannot give life an extension
cannot distance you from death
cannot reconsolidate your debt

so weak its reflex
weakened by arrows

it was flowing underground
and tossing outside
with dancing waves

my voice is now my eyes
tired of seeing
my voice is now my ears
weary of listening

my voice is now my mouth
untangled from taste
my voice is not a voice anymore
unmelted words
frozen in perennial sleep
and no flowers will rise

In an old Canadian trunk

to Luca

there are old newspapers with today's titles
and a book of outdoor life
enveloped in dust and dark
a postcard of a giftless english christmas
sprinkled with polluted carols and
and a wooden goose
which seems turned into
a pillar of salt by boredom
the open wings stalled
over the sameness
there is a small accordion
whose music ended after the
hundredth beer
a doll, there's always a doll
whose hands have scars
whose lips are covered by the great snow
of 1889
a pair of gloves for hands lost in
ivory hymnals
and a journal of accounts
where you added wrinkles
deducting days
the smell
only the smell is the same
of any old trunk hiding the
horror of all who lose their eyes
in the endless quest
along the endless mile

Burning in my remaining years

Neither heat
nor cold
slip unnoticed down
my skin

they both leave a mark
a crying or
smirking wrinkle

my age is the age of
repentance
and I will burn in my
fearful and domesticated
remaining years

shrinking and stretching
like the space
between the wings of a
butterfly

Passport size photograph

The photograph on my passport is more extraneous to me than my image in the mirror, more unpredictable than advice, more refractory than Ungaretti's stone of San Michele, more irreversible than a used match, more unsolvable than the white sheet. I am not talking about the future that has already gone. In the photograph is a me who was and is not anymore—therefore I am no longer the person who appears with a part of my already thin hair cut off by the shortsighted scissors of the photographer. It's not me because I have never been. That face belongs to other professions, other stories, other lives in other galaxies. The photographer should think, before taking pictures, about the responsibilities of his profession. To take a deontologically correct picture, the photographer should ask for a criminal record, an anamnesis and a 25/30 line max. , small biography. And, if it is possible, a series of photographs taken previously by less scrupulous colleagues of his. You are laughing at a pathetic face that cannot be mine, imagine it could be yours ... we are laughing at a person's face that does not exist ... perhaps it is dead.

Euphemism

Sunflowers, withered sunflowers. Dead. It is not usual. They are not ordinary flowers. They bend like American willows with big beehive faces—the stems still erect, like rusty drills and then the broken neck. Did you leave them on purpose? I mean there, on the table, to say that we have fought and we are approaching our withering, our wrinkling. They heavily occupy a good part of the table in that jaundiced pot. One cannot but notice them. Nobody says a word. Perhaps you didn't even see them because I am the only one for you. I should be flattered but what I feel is just a pure sensation of decadence joined to a bad odour. To get rid of it I should smell the water of the sunflowers. Maybe you have left them there just as you didn't make the bed, as you didn't flush the toilet, as I didn't shave or shower. We are the only ones. Imagine if we bent our heads as though our necks could not hold the weight of thinking about decadence and death. Imagine if we were in the yellowish pot and the sunflowers were sitting at the table wondering whether to throw us away. I remember only one literary reference about sunflowers and it is Rimbaud pissing in front of them. I like the pissing thing. It is majestic. But I won't talk about it to you because it is not the day. It's a Sunday, a weekend day, a holiday with death.

The poet was wrong

The poet was wrong.
With death in thousands
the thoughts crammed
multiplied in postcards of architecture
and landscapes
drowned in fiery water.

The poet was wrong.
Separation unplugged memory
eroding monuments carried away
through streams of debris.

The poet was wrong.
Books shook up in fire
and children queued
in assembly lines
eyes, games,
teeth and embraces
ripped off.

The poet was wrong.
Burning pyre of remembrances
to tear the darkness with learning
burning the wings of childhood
to protect the purity of ourselves.

The poet is wrong.

In a glass box

to Tom Thompson

once the old palette lies
under a sky of glass
it cannot tell us much
the choice remains mysterious
the colours drowned in a muddy whirlpool
all of them
like a collective suicide in a river
in the end the palette is a corpse
it is difficult to believe that the blood
the bark of the birch tree
the smiling face of the snow
the lingering leaf undecided
between the passion of the wind and the
affection of the stream
were all in it
in the end what remains of us
lies faded at the bottom of the river

Father

to Carlo

whoever claims that history repeats itself
doesn't accept the stuttering of existence
we too escaped from burning Troy
I miserrimus Aeneas
without offspring
on your ancient shoulders
watching the smoke
climbing up the sky

The Dowry of Education

Lá Lá libellule que fais-tu?
Lá Lá libellule veux-tu
faire du ski ou veux-tu aller
au lit?

Lá Lá libellule qu' est-ce que
ton choix!

Andrea

My memories at four years old

eating soap thinking it was macaroni
pinching the bum of my landlady's niece
in the rented summer house at the seaside
(I hated her dialect)
beating the weaker and being beaten by the stronger
my ivory elephant stolen while I slept at daycare
swimming out to the open sea and being caught by the lifeguard
holding feces while vacationing in the mountains
fondness for candles in the church
swearing when I was hungry
crying for the tie salesman kicked out of our house
holding my father's hand
being whipped by Elio who died in Africa
my sister telling me fables of slaughtered pigs
just to make me cry
my mother teaching me to read
casting a stone on Patrizia's head
organizing the great escape from school at six years old

No excessive noise after 9:00 p.m.
(the anti-noise bylaw No. 44 – 75 shall be enforced)

No warplanes flying or helicopters floating
to an ambush from the autistic sky
there is a swing kicked from its roots
two empty gums bleeding in the sand
the trucks roar orders
bouncing back and forth
across the besieged playground
the greedy cranes shake their necks
screening the surroundings
while motionless unarmed children
watch the lunar landscape

then it is silence and the machines
like exhausted mammals
hiss from the corners of
the erased playground

the leftovers lay on the concrete
tablecloth of the square—
some rubble and
sea-less and castle-free sand

there's always curiosity around
eviction
there are always kids watching and
old men remembering a past world
where destroyed playgrounds
are redolent of books
of people
and of the drilled skin of the land

Five years old

It began with me feeling you
curled up
into cloudy blue pillows

my gaze scrolling over your
sprouty face

caressing your tundra hair
bowing at the uncorrupted line
of life
the perfection of an unconscious work

and suddenly it was fear
of having to explain
the inexplicable

I was blinded
by your lips fireflying
through the black sleep

god help me

it began feeling you curl
it ended with the moon
rising at dawn

Blue cake of dreams

to Andrea

Sleep little treasure
your snowy blankets
have the consistent passion
of the wave
the very eternity of the landslide

sleep until morning
tomorrow your blue birthday cake
will remind you
of the obtuseness of your weight
and the coquetry of the sky

for you can't know the ordeal

green is your colour
of choice or brown for
we
crawling like ants
on the earthly skull
are condemned to watch
the forbidden blue
scarred by the crown of flowers
and tired arrows of grass

you are kicking walls of air
sleep castaway
from the titans' land
resume your travel
stowaway of life

you will be taught
the language of cannibals

someone will inform you
that you are a dormant volcano
that the cicadas' song
dies in the fall

how cruel
teaching is
I beg for your forgiveness
while kissing the soles
of your sleepless little feet

The dowry of education

Shhh' is chatting with herself
a self made of an echoing sphincter and
the snowy body nesting her feces

between singing and replying
there is a treasure
a pure astral smell
of fresh excrement

Shhh' is upstairs sitting on the toilet
engraving the souls of
vegetables sucked and titillated

she is leading her caravel
to the world of poo poo fables and
treasures of golden caca . . .

. . . we were equals
before life
Andrea and I

learning and guilt
are the dowry of education
papá . . . papá

pa-pá—poo-poo
I finally see
the link of my sperm

with the letter p
so fatherhood
is about our sphincters

our learning of the
alphabetical defecation
finally we talk to each other

Playing

To Oscar

Jumping over the blocks of Stonehenge
or hopping from nadir to zenith
through mysterious points
marked on the sidewalks

you peterpan from sneaking clouds
you can fly without hovering
you make poetry without dreaming

in you yourself
you open your wings

We call you Rose Petal

the playground has been erased
my child is stirring the sand
like a gentle hurricane

there are only basketball players
and dope smokers
postdamer platz hangers
hidden in the corners
of the concrete entrances
doors of wind and dope
first sex first aid
we are alone
Andrea and I
where are the other children?

she pulls from the sand
a chocolate cake
where the dog was spinning
seagulls fight for leftover *masa*
and pasta
sparrows and pigeons
learn about hierarchy

where are the other children?
for me the sand is the hand of the sea
for you it is the whole universe

our memories don't collide
my memories don't enlighten you
yours are beyond the clouds
the bridge of the milky way
is inaccessible to me

I love you with my smallness
you are life for an illness
your solitude is mine
mine the sins mine the guilt
emerging from your sand
which you stir like a gentle hurricane

Grace Schoolyard

what is a Cuban sky?
it is the wide cloudless sky
of Manitoba

watching . . .
a school
built in mute concrete
its belligerant presence softened
by realist touches of jaundiced yellow
and swimming pool blue

an elementary school with many
and small windows
like East Berlin or Cuba
where quantity prevails over quality

it's a typical exercise during illness
never forgotten but hidden intermittently
by the scent of lake weed and by the acute skirmishes
of pigeons and seagulls

the head of a cynical horizon
faints with an abrupt fall
guillotined by sharp roofs

into the lake
a shy and insipid Goliath
compared to the salty Davidic sea
it is happening here

constantly happening here
under the engraved pupils
of a hungry seagull
bowing
over the socialist roof
of the school

now everything seems still
Andrea filling buckets
with slow biblical wisdom
the barking of a dog
brought by the wind
rides a cloud with the bell-sound

of the distant catholic church
only death keeps working
it is complicated
formal and
let's admit it
bureaucratic
it is never superficial
killing is superficial

We were not the first nations
(we are not the first we are not the last)

Andrea it is preposterous but I imagined
landmarks remembering
where you set your foot
crystallized snapshots of you and
your mother at the crossroads of
the city

I wonder if our embracing
could be linotyped in a thousand copies
because I have always been fearful
of my fear of forgetting

it is preposterous
I am dreaming of a world where
I have never lived
a parallel world where
too much has been said and
written

anthem: if these domestic borders
could all dance for birth
and these lands
could evergreen
unconscious of seasons and
time

if the love songs
and the lullabies
could silence and bury
the rhetoric of fatherhood
the fear of being forgotten

then the echo of repentance
would mimic the last breath
of the dying soldier who sees
children playing on the line of the horizon

Spies in Kensington

to Deborah

Your suburban upbringing
drove me to the downtown of your hearth

Souvenir

the air smelling of sperm
a laundry breath
wakes up
the sidewalks

if I could stop
the blossoming tree
of my memory
whose branches

pierce my skin
whose leaves tickle
my cheek bones
my sphincter

*

this turtle shield
roof of sweet watermelon
these sandy seeds these tired clothes
these cheap toys
these working boots this luggage
miss you

*

you and I are watched by the thousand eyes
of snappers
crabs
sardinhas
and lobsters

my loving you
is concave
the rain of naughty Leonides

your loving me
is the dive of the scavenger
the rostrum of the galley

we will end up
like that
loving each other by ourselves

*

it rained a lot
in those days
we slid along
the windows

we left paths of
slime on the glass
until we laid on
wet sheets

we erected with sperm
and humour the walls
for our protection

you were a butterfly before . . .
before my petals opened for you
before the breeze invited you to dance

*

death comes from the road to Emmaus
to give us the last miracle

I will trace a circle of sperm
around your body
I will pray to God
with a rosary of orgasm

we are not in the world
your humours
trace the only known road
unknown to us

Large two forms

a sculpture by Henry Moore

balcony of love
fossilized sponge
musical doughnut

on your whitened dark membrane
little Juliets
draw lines of boredom

balcony of love
fossilized sponge
musical doughnut

through the arches of your sternum
whispered dreams and waitings
embrace the wind

another streetcar is arriving

Lovers

I have seen them kissing . . .
him and her . . . while the
capricious wind
ruffled hair and
caressed timid flowers

I have seen them
climb the stairs to that garret
where the most daring branches
knocked gently at the glass
of the only window

the lovers don't sleep
the lovers don't pray
the lovers don't work
the lovers don't bathe
sometimes they shop
sometimes they remember the seasons
and their nocturnal sounds
are those of playful bats

one night he woke up and offered his
luminous body to the moon
who wanted to abduct him
she crowned his wings and
he stayed
one night she woke up
and she offered herself as a cloud
to the desire of the wind
but he embraced her and
she stayed

the lovers don't sleep
the lovers don't hope
the lovers don't work
the lovers don't bathe
sometimes they shop
sometimes they remember the seasons
and their nocturnal sounds
are those of playful bats

that winter I saw them ... the lovers ...
they had not aged
he didn't shave
she didn't wash her hair
they no longer worked
they kissed behind the misted over window
which separated them from the world
I went out in the morning
and came back at night
the lovers felt the cold
they felt the heat
but didn't remember
sometimes they woke up at night
and walked outside
their footprints laid on the snow
sometimes his are ahead of hers
sometimes hers are ahead of his
but they are always joined
and when they went back
their garret was shining
and the silently falling snow
kept them awake

the lovers look at me from the window
of a garret in a city
that goes to bed with me at night
and wakes up in the morning
a city that hopes
that doesn't sleep
that shops
that works
that grows old
that doesn't run away
that dies

I have seen them kissing
while the last wintry wind
tepidly ruffled their hair . . .
the lovers. . . .

Cockroach
Perplaneta Americana

chez Mars
I love stewed prunes
the stones gathered in a little saucer
look like abortions of cockroaches

I resemble more and more
my father
with his nose hair willowing
over the lip
and his wattles
that I used to stare at

when I was a kid I believed
that my father
lost his jaw in the war

here at Mars
there are no retired teachers
nibbling slowly and quoting
old dead languages
just lonesome TTC employees

there's a nasty chef
turning bacon
as if he was punching the bag
and an idiot of a waiter
always smiling
and saying:
tonight I have this and I have that and what would you like?

the only things he could claim to own are
his dumb eyes
you are sitting close to me
and perhaps you are watching me
I have forgotten about you

I am looking at the bacon
when I realize you are looking at me
and I look at the Macedonian chef
who wanted to be a boxer

I can feel my stomach pressing against
the button of my coat
it is like a solitary hero
against the charge of dyspepsia

you are so beautiful
that I cannot tell you
that the prune stones
look like abortions of cockroaches
without those little legs
and those antennas

you cannot defeat the cockroaches
I know and I am thinking
that the prunes will ignite a cleansing process
in my stomach

that's the usual train of thought at Mars
in the evening

we talk about the weather
at night in this diner where time is relative
sitting at the counter
close to an employee of the TTC
and at the other side there's a chef
the ex-boxer
an optimistic waiter
and another one spooning rice pudding

I who am a night hawk
I have only the bags
under my eyes
and my father's wattles
and you
who are pregnant
and so beautiful
you are really beautiful
I cannot tell you
that these prune stones
look like abortions of cockroaches
how can I tell you?

Toponymy and Environs

(pharmacological journal drafted by a drug addict who went into withdrawal in a monastery on the Bracco hills.)

to Stefania and Emilia

Methadone[1] Epthadone[2]

Indications:
here we are at the delta of sebum.
a head that stinks like feet.
drunk on helium
in a hotel with foggy rooms
and dumpy carpet lined corridors
the flaring exit
standing out like a buoy in a dark ocean.

we became talking totems
of wisdoms.
travels and canvasses and dreams
and virus
choked together
in the chemical slipknot
of terror and dignity.

some confused memories of linguistic souvenirs
slip away from the eddy of
nostalgia.
the mods' era
the suburban commuting
from epthadone, thalidomide and cyanide
to the Bracco hills.

Directions:
in the vein
in the mouth
in your fists
shears of freedom
for work family mortgage.
the last hours of sleep waiting for
the syrup
yawns of glucose
and mimesis with leaves.

for we want to fall too
in season
and live again
by season.

Caution:
skin changing in a coalescence
of rules and customs.

Warning:
immediate repentance and an uncontrollable
tendency to confide
on up to the realm of snitching.
in case of a heavy crisis please consult a physician.

Morphine 3

Indications:
the presence of another woman
in a monastery of fathers, Passionists.
another virgin wandering along the hills.
a smile like a bonfire over dead agricultural hamlets.

a tree blossoming inside the body.
branches like vessels radiate from brain to feet
from sphincter to genitals.
in this station we see one crucified
on the clouds.

Directions:
during compline the choir of fierce Passionists
envelopes the monastery.
the bleak hills
appear numb to the music of the fog.

Caution:
it's all the fault of emigration
abandoned villages.
seniors endlessly watching the shallow landscape
and smoking cigarettes without filters.
the old pharmacists rummage through their closets.
substances hidden in liberty box cases.
the drug's names drawn by Beardsley.

and the prayers for death
with no resurrection
cannot do anything to quench
dry ampoules like dry breasts.
the ash of the virgin
conserved in a mausoleum of glass.

Warning:
next time I shall not be a lizard
or a magpie.

Opium 4

Directions:
mercenary training ship.
coarse senile language.
the mother of all sins.
the apple of new gardens.

Warning:
eating it is like
injecting the eucharist.

Caution:
the opposite of Attila
it destroys itself inside
burning veins and papillae
as if they were green fields.

friends were withdrawing in
the swamps
they didn't want to hear his name
or taste his sword.

Cocktail 5

the humid
lime slobbers
on the brick-molecular
wall's
anonyrnous
and tottering structure.

Indications:
we are in the
damp and grey basement
of a one storey house.
dreams and genealogical trees
bundled for winter.

Warning:
graffiti.
telephone numbers
and stains
resembling excrement.
outside naked piers and hooks
of unfinished constructions.
lands for speculation.

. . . of cerebral ischemia.
Giovanni is dying and
screaming that bulls
want to break down the gate.

Non-medicinal ingredients:
even Enrico who
hides wine in his locker
where the nuns always find it
will die soon.
he lies mute on the bed with
the face of an old waiter
waiting for orders.

suburban cirrhosis
already seen
already heard.

Caution:
was alchemy ever able to create
the philosophers' stone?

Catapresan[6]

Warning:
the roar of the winds
gathered by Eolus
in his goliard expeditions.
the vault of the wave that sinks
the desecrator Diomedes.
the tanks that crash the barricade.
meager resistance of four intellectuals and
a hundred lumpen
blinded by illusions.

Directions:
cata and presan
cata cata
aboriginal war scream and
presan
an enthusiastic "god in us."
STOP THE BULLS. STOP THEM.
THEY ARE COMING 'R COMING!
the bulls the bulls
the ischemic hints of a veronica
staggering in the chaos of the herd.

Counterindications:
sound of the sea crashing against the dura mater.

Novocaine 7

Directions:
an experiment by a young doctor Mengele
in a hospital in Liguria.
modified spring of benzoic goddess.

Warning:
flung beyond the moon
vaguely seen
launched into the gelid atmosphere
where even silence is a scream.

Counterindications:
smoking and watching yourself
laying in bed
afraid of dwarfs behind the door

afraid of the wooden horse
whose bowels hide cop squads.
tattooing the bed sheets
with the cigarette.
time passing by in bed
and/or in front of the mirror
sometimes picking up the telephone
to cross the water
on the shoulders of a frog.

watching your dick
then television
then your dick
then television

and always mumbling
if if if if if
like the old man
who lost the war.

Valium[8]

<u>Directions</u>:
hence you take a couple of vials
and fill up a 10cc syringe.
you suck and listen
you listen and suck the milk of relief.

<u>Warning</u>:
like a flask of red wine in your veins
the flow of goodness invades your eyes
a stuttering of salient moments
sweetens your corneas.
the first shot
the first book
the second shot
the second book . . .
he who is listening is the compassionate
passenger met at the tavern
at the station
at the hospital.
you are sorry for yourself
and you want everybody to cry for you.
the nurses ask you
and now do you feel better?
but you can only feel sadness mounting over you . . .
because the world is riding you and tears
are not enough
to clean up the ward
or to sweep the stables.
you shall fall asleep until the
bartender wakes you up
shouting at you that he must close.
then the nurse tucks you into bed
and whispers in dialect
shaking her head.

nobody will sleep tonight.
Enrico is gone
after a long lament
on board a submarine.
he has been swallowed up by
an ocean of wine.

Roipnol[9]

Warning:
let it walk ahead of you
never go ahead of it.
hence all motor activities
must stop.
one needs to lie down and
wait with no hurry.
in this game of cat and mouse
do not try to escape.
humour the quick paw.
pay attention.
you can hear its steps.
it will turn you over
it will examine you
it will withdraw and
it will come back.
humour it for its needs are
those of the hunter . . .
breathe on its predator fur . . .
your fear gives it pleasure . . .

Counterindications:
if you fight it
the predator
will enter in you and
you will become insatiable
you'll salivate because
you'll need a victim.
in the shade of therapies there is neither
cool
nor relief.

Heroin[10]

Warning:
contemplation of no place.
titillation of negative space.
replacement of the sky
with blue water
from the bottom of the bathtub.

Indications:
industrial archeology.
revitalization of industrial sites.
underground twinnings
the option par excellence.

the basement
the garret
the landing
the hovel
the house in construction
the house in demolition
the young mould
the old mould.

Speedball[11]

Indications:
pendular game.
competition of purity.
cocaine & heroin united in a white wedding.
banned from olympus
in front of the spelean people.

they consummated after eyeing each other
for a long time
and they never left each other.

Counterindications:
nails and fangs
stuck in their niveous flesh.

Notes

1. Methadone: synonymous with chicory coffee, inflatable dolls, cultured pearls.

2. Epthadone: see methadone

3. Morphine: *M'illumino d'immenso—I grow radiant/in the immensity of it all* (Giuseppe Ungaretti—translated by Diego Bastianutti)

4. Opium: war and flowers don't work well together but nowadays war and poppies reconnect in the best of the traditions.

5. Cocktail: an ineffective blend of drugs designed to fight addiction.

6. Catapresan: drug used to treat epilepsy and to fight addiction.

7. Novocaine: gum masturbation.

8. Valium: kitchen drug.

9. Roipnol: hypnotic aimed at resolving all the problems in the world.

10. Heroin: is there anything that has not been said or written about the subject?

11. Speedball: interracial marriage: cocaine + heroin or morphine + amphetamine or . . .

Tonight I am the State

to all my friends in Milan

this queue is drawing my blood
like the mosquito of the dawn
this rum is discolouring desire
only the cheek of the child is paler than this milk
even today this line springs from promises
and ends up with history

I have learnt to entertain myself with useless questions
is the queue longer than the waiting?
is the waiting longer than the queue?
is hope begotten by the fight or the fight begotten by hope?
is it better to be in good health or to be free?
the faces of the missing
of those who have attempted the ocean
are not painted on the walls

José Antonio Ernesto Camilito
in my sole dream
there is a gate to heaven
though it could be hell
without a queue
without libreta
if you were not here I'd feel lonelier
than the crab in the middle of the road
his claws lifted against the indifferent tire

the fear that all our dead
our heroes
if they were alive
would tell us to resist

just like when I hit your chest
don't come before me
hold on! hold on!
think about him!

think about the Lider Maximo
against the Americans

but if I think about him
I'll come too soon

then think about the dead!
our dead
remember Frank Pais remember Abel Santamaria
remember Camilo Cienfuegos
remember Che
Hatuey
José Martí

imagine the gods waking up inside the palms
and beating along the drum tree
blood leaks in tears scenting History

think about the slaughter of the pigs
about the gold which ran out
leaving a bitter taste
think about the breath of gall sweetened by
the tobacco leaf

about the armoured train blowing up in anger

let's root love
because the heat glues us for hours
and we unglue with free trajectories
you are the cuntpiercing cormorant
I am the peniscatcher falcon
while screams with hooks and beaks
resound in this room
shreds colouring the walls
into a large magna square
where we fly over you
asshole smeller
then I descend on a branch
and I dance waiting to fall asleep
waiting for the bat's singing

(ready or not, here I come . . .)
a life under embargo
is like a fly zipped forever
a sea that carries only to the coast
a plane which only lands and never leaves

we who were born with the embargo
cannot distinguish the outside from the inside
it is a voice from birth
growing despite the queue the libreta
the dead the gods
despite your love for me
the heat and the mosquitoes
it is the slap of the wave whipping itself

ready or not
here I come

the malnourished dancers dismantle the set of Giselle
and they go to the Tropicana and dance with the tourists
lured by the illusion the prince dances to death
the slave wins the slaver
hugging the tourist
all this movement makes me hungry

History will absolve me
nothing more boring
than Moros y Cristianos
it is like watching an action movie
at Cubavision
where heroes are cane cutters
peasants are philosophers of the local cell
and heroes never shut up

rice and beans
at Radiorebelde the uncommitted rotten youth
take drugs in Colombia
whore out in Puerto Rico

dignity in black and white
the country sits at the table
Moros y Cristianos
the balsero approaches the coral customs

despacio
the warrior
who left children and conflicts
who headed to the hundred fires
was terminated by the leprosy
he wanted to cure
he lays on a pallet portrayed by the local Mantegna

lost battles became miracles
his evangelic writings
were traded and altered into apocrypha

now his face is impressed
on a thousand shrouds
his body buried somewhere
and so many are waiting for his return

the breeding of Varadero
like each imperial morning
the crooked and wrinkled laborers
were waiting for Monsieur Dupont
who was late
they spat

I am hanging around with a little bit of money
among breeding bulls and cows to be bred
I am waiting for the results of the blood test
I must wait for a month at least
I'll call up the doctor once I'm at home

I have left Alvadys with unavoidable doubts
you almost engineer without ruler
without pads

Heiida you are hiding your sole condom
in your bra
you'll keep it alive like an old Chevy
you'll turn it out and you'll turn it in

you are not my Friday
you told me that after three days
I would not remember your face

I am your State
tonight I am your Lider Maximo

I kidnapped you
goat cow pig
grown in the dark
you gauging the thickness of my dick
to forecast the time of my departure

you write me that you got married and you have a child
grown in the dark
the son of periodo especial
you are so distant so discoloured
that your letters seem epigraphs

sleep old pontiac sleep my esposa
I loved you more than any woman
like a woman you had colours and sounds

we were together
in the countryside on the mountain at the seaside
in Pinar in Havana in Santa Clara
in Camaguey
in VARADERO
you are so counterrevolutionary that
you loved and have begotten children without ideologies

sucio is the sea, filthy, rotten
despite a blue smile
this water wicked with attrition
coitus
coral phalluses
humorous jelly fishes
mobile foams
tears of rum
horizons of concrete

this sea to wear
like an invisible cloak
fills up buddies and pals
vaginas assholes mouths
rubs the eyes
steals their colour

burns like Deianira's tunic
like the flame of Hatuey
with the fire that the pyre cannot extinguish
the pain of farewell

tonight I am the State
that night my senses were jamming
the bed sheet restlessly fluctuating
smell of milk
pouring from her armpits
from her lavic breast

then her curls sprouted from
the white ploughed pillow
thin and shining waves
blown by a timid moon

her eyelids were gates for the bull
her lips were the quicksand of forgiveness
but her hands
were not curious
not voracious

tonight I am the State
Moros y Cristianos
I am bartering an old drunken boat
and American dollars
for your shining sprouts

we bite our breath in the silence

it was me it was you
sea animals in the sunset
you emerging from the silent sky-struck sea

your belly still beating in a far country

walk, keep walking
wait
wait and walk

the breathing of the exhausted engine
has stopped
walk until the victory
walk to Havana

wait for the truck loading
the doctors the peasants the workers
walk to the horizon
to the unattainable victory
to the imperial customs

you were born like the god inside a palm
and inside a palm you have grown up
spying on men and animals

you have waited for the barbarians
the counter-revolutionaries

sentinel
you pretended to be asleep in a barrack
emasculated by playa Giron and Escambray
you had screened the horizon of asphalt

in your dream you are surrounded by the worms of Mariel
by balseros by jineteras

you are smiling
because you are holding a flaming sword
angel of an exhausted god

Sierra
you've asked for help from everybody
and you've helped everybody
your love has been defended
and profaned
by men in different uniforms
regular irregular soldiers
conquistadores barbudos
moros y cristianos u indios
their wishes burn out
their bodies punished by dreams and clouds

your herbs have cured asthma
your eyes have diagnosed the fevers
your arms have dug the graves of the dead

you've undone the canvas
and concede yourself to no one

S.S.Granma
we are still on our journey
and aren't you tired
of all these weary warriors?
Aeneas is crossing his fingers
Roland has sold his Durendal

the poet tunes his lyre
he is not singing of the repentance
he sings of the rejected counter-revolution
the sacrifice of life

he sings of blood and sweat
without any skill or trade
(and when did he have any? because he had thousands)

even today
there's no land on the horizon
the poet cannot see
he is counting the wrinkles of silence
(I am still alive May 18)

Cuba
in charge of universal responsibility
I in a little field
pushing the ploughshare
what a life is life
when the moon on the clear sea
round and fat
pale and whimsical

fantasizes
and begs standing at the corner of a cloud
and then she goes and rests
deaf to my pains

I am lonely in the island of poverty and nature
ahi! the trumpet of the sun is pushing
breakfast time and cigars
one   two   three
I am in charge of universal responsibility

you bartered the Hippocratic oath
for a box of ammunition

your motorbike blocked by the
Periodo Especial

you could drive for nations and continents
death has dueled with you
perhaps you thought you could win
and for your arrogance she
has cut off your hands

Nuestra America
to me the Indies are a few miles away
between the sea and the dream

I know that our dead
will not approve
searching like sentinels the sea customs
the arrival of the felucca and of the airplane
greeting the foreign delegation that brings
precious spices and monsters

the country moans and bleeds with
interrupted orgasms

you hug me and like picaflores
we take the pleasure of limited ellipsis
if you were not here
with me I'd forget
health
education
the country and the Sierra

because Cuba is an island
island of zafra
of absolution of libreta and querida presencia

but the sea
scented with freedom and flight
is a concrete trunk
it is a hero and a betrayer
it is alive and cemeterial

Nuevitas
my house is not here
not here where the pale beaches
blind the tourist with beauty
and the palms are confessionals of the sun god

my house is where love
is scented by the jewels of Yemayá
my house is in a little harbour
in a queue for a Changó-bleeding flat bread
in the open sewers where extroverted rats live
and where rapacious mosquitoes fly
in a torrid theatre
the toy of erudite conquistadores
defeated by little blue princes and little dancing princesses

it is here where I am
it is here that I am not I
where silence obeys different rules
from 2:00 p.m. to 4:00 p.m.

and one dies
in the afternoon in Nuevitas
it is here where I would like to live
not to be a *real man*
not to be a *new man*
just to rest from all those years spent looking for you
to sleep without interrupted dreams
to listen to the sea knocking at the door

here is my house

Notes

Libreta: Rationing card.

Hatuey: The Indian leader, Hatuey, tried to organize a rebellion against the Spanish in the 1530s. He was captured and burned alive.

Tropicana: The famous cabaret in Havana.

History will absolve me: After his capture in the attack on Moncada barracks in Santiago, Fidel Castro was put on trial. Castro defended himself. His defence speech is known to history by its concluding line, "History will absolve me."

Moros y Cristianos: National Cuban dish—rice and beans.

Balseros: People trying to flee Cuba by sailing on rafts.

Jineteras: Young Cuban prostitutes—the word may mean horse rider.

Periodo Especial: After the fall of the Soviet Union the Cuban government initiated a "Special Period" in 1990 of harsh new austerity measures and hardship to be borne by the large majority of Cubans.

Nuestra America: Title of a famous essay by José Martí.

Picaflor: Sort of a Cuban hummingbird.

Zafra: The harvest of the sugar cane.

Yemayá: The Goddess Orisha (Cuban syncretic cult—goddess of the Nigerian culture Yoruba—Santeria).

Changó/Shangó: The God Orisha, master of lightning.

The real man: The man described by José Martí in his essays. A new kind of figure embodying the Indian, the black and the white man.

The new man: The man idealized by Che Guevara.

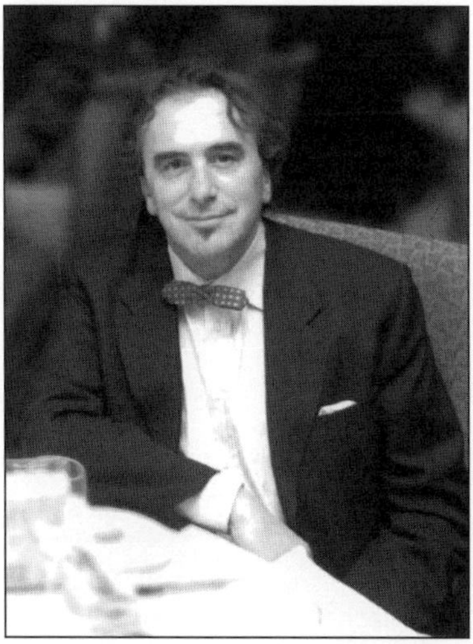

Corrado Paina was born in Milan, Italy in 1954 and he has lived in Toronto, Canada since 1987. *The Dowry of Education* is his fifth book.